Contents

What are grains?

seeds

Grains are the seeds from some plants.

Eating grains can keep us healthy.

wheat

rice

Wheat and rice are grains.

oats

Oats are grains.

Food from grains

rice

We cook some grains before eating.

flour

We make some grains into flour.

pasta

bread

Bread and pasta are made
from flour.

tortilla

Some tortillas are made from flour.

How grains help us

Eating grains and potatoes gives you energy.

You need energy to work and play.

part of the grain

Some foods are made with part of the grain.

whole grain

Some foods are made with the whole grain.

Eating whole grains helps your body fight illness.

Eating whole grains helps keep your heart healthy.

Healthy eating

We need to eat different kinds of food each day.

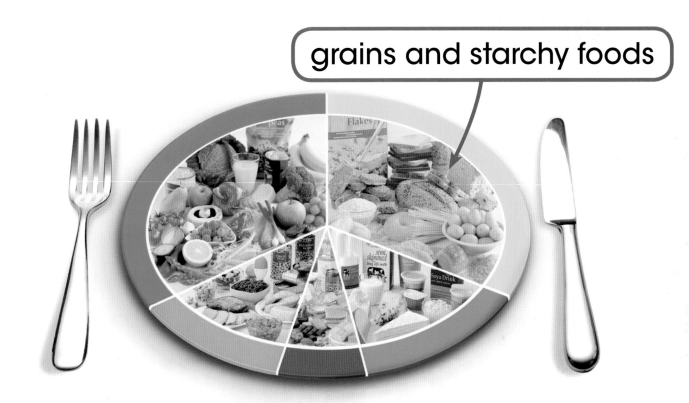

grains and starchy foods

The eatwell plate shows us which foods to eat.

We eat grains and potatoes to stay healthy.

We eat grains and potatoes because they taste good!

Find the grains

Here is a healthy dinner. Can you find a food made from grains?

Answer on page 24

Picture glossary

 **energy** the power to do something. We need energy when we work or play.

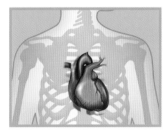 **heart** part of your body inside your chest. Your heart pushes blood around your body.

 **seed** plants make seeds. Seeds grow into new plants. We can eat some seeds.

Index

Answer to quiz on page 22: The bread is made from grains.

Notes for parents and teachers

Before reading

Explain that we need to eat a range of different foods to stay healthy. Splitting foods into different groups can help us understand how much food we should eat from each group. Show the starchy food section of the plate on page 19. Starchy foods are foods that give us energy. About a third of the food we eat should be starchy food. Grains are seeds from plants. Wheat is a grain that we use to make starchy foods, such as bread or pasta. Other starchy foods include potatoes, cereal, and rice.

After reading

• Play spot the starchy food. Take children around a supermarket in small groups and get them to draw or record all the starchy foods they see. Alternatively, hold up pictures of different types of food and get the children to indicate when they think a starchy food is being shown.

• Discuss the difference between foods made with whole grain (literally the entire grain kernel) such as brown bread, and foods where part of the grain has been removed, such as white flour, white bread, and white rice. Explain that whole grain foods are much better for us. Bring in three different types of whole wheat bread (checking that no children have gluten allergies). Conduct a taste test to see which kind of bread is the favourite.

• Help the children to each design a healthy lunch (or lunch box). Discuss the sorts of things that might go into a healthy lunch and the importance of including a range of different types of food. What starchy food are they going to include? The lunches could be drawn on paper plates and displayed along with a drink for each meal.